chocolate

* A SWEET INDULGENCE

KARL PETZKE AND SARA SLAVIN

PHOTOGRAPHY:
KARL PETZKE

ART DIRECTION, STYLING:
SARA SLAVIN

TEXT:
CAROLYN MILLER

DESIGN:
MORLA DESIGN

RECIPES, FOOD STYLING:
SANDRA COOK

CHRONICLE BOOKS
SAN FRANCISCO

Printed in Hong Kong.

Library of Congress Cataloging-in-Publication Data:
Petzke, Karl. Chocolate: a sweet indulgence/ by
Karl Petzke and Sara Slavin; text by Carolyn Miller;
recipes by Sandra Cook; design by Morla Design, Inc.
p. cm.
Includes bibliographical references (p.).
ISBN 0-8118-1592-7 (hc).
ISBN 0-8118-1591-9 (pbk.)
1. Cookery (Chocolate) 2. Chocolate. I. Slavin, Sara.
II. Miller, Carolyn. III. Title.
TX767.C5P48 1997
641.3'374–dc20   96-28605
                    CIP

Book and cover design:
Morla Design, Inc., San Francisco

Distributed in Canada by Raincoast Books
8680 Cambie Street
Vancouver, B.C. V6P 6M9

10 9 8 7 6 5 4 3 2 1

Chronicle Books
85 Second Street
San Francisco, CA 94105

Web Site: www.chronbooks.com

CONTENTS

CREDITS

Excerpt from the foreword to *The Gastronomical Me* in *The Art of Eating* by M. F. K. Fisher. Reprinted with the permission of Macmillan Publishing Company.

Excerpt from "Why I Am Not a Buddhist" in *Original Love* by Molly Peacock. Reprinted with the permission of W. W. Norton & Company.

Excerpt from *Charlie and the Chocolate Factory* by Roald Dahl. Reprinted with the permission of Penguin Books USA, Inc.

"If Chocolate," by Susan Herron Sibbet, from *Burnt Toast and Other Recipes*. Reprinted with the permission of White Mountain Press.

ACKNOWLEDGEMENTS

Collaboration is a sweet thing; a conduit for creativity. The people below have our heartfelt gratitude for all they have done.

Nion McEvoy, Michael Carabetta, Christina Wilson, and the staff at Chronicle Books for once again providing unfailing support.

Jennifer Morla for working her magic on these words and photos with patience, flexibility and great style.

Carolyn Miller for her sweet words: always knowing what to say and how to say it.

Sandra Cook for recipes both daring and delicious and for styling them with charm and creativity.

Craig Bailey and the great staff at Morla Design for their ongoing support. Allyson Levy, Vicki Roberts Russell, and Ann Tonai for assisting with recipe testing and food styling. Wendi Nordeck for photo assisting.

Iris Fuller, Robert Perez and the staff at Fillamento, Sue Fisher King and the staff at Sue Fisher King, and Naomi at Naomi's Antiques To Go for their generosity in allowing us to use their beautiful things.

Robert Voorhees and Dr. Robert Steinberg for their guidance, kindness, and chocolate expertise.

Jim Walsh of Hawaiian Vintage Chocolate for his generosity and support.

The chocolatiers of France: Michel Chaudon, and La Maison du Chocolat in Paris, and Matthieu Barès at Bernachon in Lyon.

George Dolese for his kindness, graciousness and great help to us in Paris.

Kathleen and Peter Van Dine and Iris and Michael Sainato for their help and support.

With my love and thanks for always being there: Mark Steisel, Sybil and Kate Slavin, and Lillian Moss. - S.S.

To my wife Mari for your kindness, love, and understanding. - K.P.

sweet

"How lovely and warm!" whispered Charlie.

"I know. And what a marvelous smell!"

answered Grandpa Joe, taking a long deep sniff.

All the most wonderful smells in the world seemed to

be mixed up in the air around them—

the smell of roasting coffee and burnt

sugar and melting chocolate and mint and violets and

crushed hazelnuts and apple blossom and caramel

and lemon peel . . .

ROALD DAHL, *CHARLIE AND THE CHOCOLATE FACTORY*

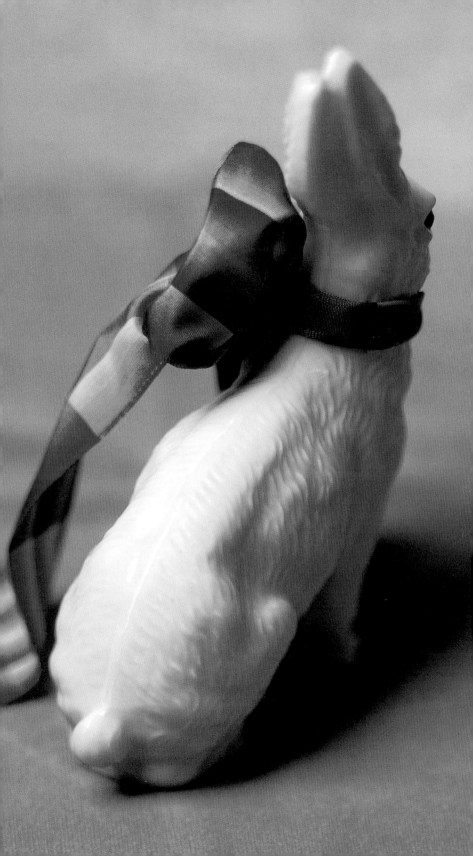

To be human is to desire. We know that animals have wants and needs and memories, but unlike us, they live almost entirely in the moment, not in the past or the future. And it is the tangled interplay between the world of memory and the world of the future that creates the human province of desire.

Of the many complex desires that civilization has fostered, almost none is so easily satisfied as the desire for chocolate. Although it has existed in edible form only since the middle of the nineteenth century, today chocolate is available in an astonishing number of forms, and the passion for it seems to be endemic to much of the Western world.

The craving for chocolate is physical, arising out of the desire for its uniquely dark, slightly bitter, rich taste; but the craving is also emotional, for chocolate symbolizes, as does no other food, luxury, comfort, sensuality, gratification, and love.

I LOVE DESIRE, THE STATE OF WANT AND
OF HOW TO GET; BUILDING A KINGDOM IN A SOUL
REQUIRES DESIRE.

MOLLY PEACOCK, FROM "WHY I AM NOT A BUDDHIST"

Pure chocolate by itself is bitter and distasteful, but an alchemy occurs when it is combined with other foods. From the earliest days of its history, chocolate was mixed with almost anything anyone could think of in order to lighten it. The Mayans and the Aztecs used chilies, cornmeal, honey, ambergris, musk, vanilla. The Europeans used pepper and other spices to flavor their chocolate, and mixed it with water and even beer and wine. No one is sure who first thought to mix chocolate with milk to serve as a warm drink; some say it was a Spanish nun in Central America, others credit an unknown English person. In any case, milk, cream, and butter, all unavailable to the Amerindians because they did not have dairy animals, would eventually make chocolate the meltingly smooth and luxurious substance that it is today.

CHOCOLATE AND CHILIES
* * *

From the time they were first ground into a paste by the Mayans, cocoa beans were mixed with ground dried chilies to counter the bitter taste of pure chocolate. This combination of foods persists in Mexican cuisine today in its ultimate version: the dark, mysterious, multilayered, and seductively earthy *mole poblano*, the mole sauce from Puebla.

CHOCOLATE AND SPICES
* * *

The Mayans added ground cinnamon, cloves, and aniseed to their chocolate, along with ground chilies. Something of this tradition persists in Mexican chocolate such as the Ibarra brand, perfumed with ground almonds and cinnamon, and sold in a distinctive yellow and red hexagonal box. A hint of nutmeg, cinnamon, cloves, or mace is sometimes added to chocolate desserts to enhance the flavor of the chocolate.

Before 2000 B.C.: COCOA TREES ARE FOUND GROWING IN THE RAIN FORESTS OF CENTRAL AMERICA BY THE MAYA INDIANS.

A.D. 600: THE MAYA CULTIVATE THE COCOA TREE IN YUCATÁN. COCOA BEANS ARE USED AS CURRENCY.

1502: CHRISTOPHER COLUMBUS FIRST TASTES COCOA IN NICARAGUA.

CHOCOLATE AND DAIRY FOODS

* * *

Mixing chocolate with other foods not only mitigates its bitterness, but makes it smoother, subtler, and more sensuous. When butter and cream were added to chocolate along with sugar, the sublime art of chocolate confectionery was born, first practiced by the French but also excelled in by the Swiss, Italians, Germans, Belgians, and Americans. The freshness and quality of the butter and cream, as well as the quality of the chocolate, determine the best chocolates. Cream is also an important ingredient in such desserts as chocolate mousse and pots de crème.

CHOCOLATE AND EGGS

* * *

Eggs and chocolate made possible the development of chocolate cakes; the first of these was the Sachertorte, still famous today for its union of thin layers of chocolate sponge cake, apricot jam, and a shining coat of ganache.

CHOCOLATE AND FRUIT

* * *

This may be the most sensuous of all food combinations. For luxury, it is hard to surpass a tart or cake that matches chocolate with fresh raspberries, except perhaps with *les poires belle Hélène*, poached pear halves topped with vanilla ice cream and warm chocolate sauce. Chocolate and bananas is a favorite American pairing, as evidenced by the banana split, one of the most American of desserts; another wonderful concoction is homemade banana-and-black-walnut ice cream, topped with chocolate sauce. America can also take credit for chocolate fondue: chunks of fresh fruit speared by long forks and skewers and dipped in a pool of warm chocolate sauce. Giant long-stemmed strawberries dipped in couverture chocolate are a classic sign of luxury on the buffets of large American hotels.

1520:
CHOCOLATE ARRIVES IN SPAIN FROM MEXICO AND BECOMES POPULAR IN THE COURT OF MADRID.
SPANISH MONKS PERFECT THE ROASTING AND GRINDING OF COCOA BEANS, MAKING THE PASTE INTO
RODS OR TABLETS FOR THE NOBILITY. SPAIN GROWS COCOA IN MEXICO AND KEEPS IT FOR ITSELF.
HEAVILY TAXED, CHOCOLATE IS PRIMARILY A DRINK OF THE NOBILITY.

CHOCOLATE - MINT POTS DE CRÈME

* * *

INCREDIBLY RICH AND SMOOTH, WITH JUST ENOUGH MINT TO COMPLEMENT BUT NOT OVERWHELM.

2 cups heavy cream

4 ounces semisweet chocolate, chopped

6 egg yolks

2 tablespoons sugar

Pinch of salt

2 teaspoons vanilla extract

2 teaspoons peppermint extract

Make sure the oven rack is in the center of the oven. Preheat oven to 325°F. Place 1 1/2 cups of the cream in a small saucepan over low heat. Place remaining 1/2 cup cream and chocolate in large double boiler over medium heat. In a medium-sized mixing bowl, stir the egg yolks until blended.

When the cream in the small saucepan is scalded (a thin skin forms on top), stir in sugar and salt and remove from heat.

Whisk the chocolate and cream in double boiler until smooth. Off the heat, slowly add scalded cream to chocolate mixture, stirring to maintain smooth texture. Slowly add this mixture to egg yolks, continuing to stir for smooth texture. Add vanilla and peppermint extracts, stirring again until mixed in. Pour entire mixture back into the double boiler, continuing to whisk over medium heat for 3 to 4 minutes.

Pour mixture into individual soufflé cups, leaving a bit of room at top. Place cups in a shallow baking pan with enough water to come halfway up side of cups. Cover baking pan with cookie sheet and bake for 25 minutes. Remove from oven and cool. Refrigerate for 1 to 2 hours before serving. Serves 8.

CHOCOLATE AND NUTS

* * *

These two earthy foods seem meant for each other, and the list of their permutations is almost as long as the list of the many kinds of nuts. Along with sugar, nuts are the source for *praliné,* the elegant filling adored by chocolatiers and chocolate lovers.

CHOCOLATE AND COFFEE

* * *

This mating reaches divine status among lovers of both chocolate and caffeine, especially since it is now widely available in the form of café mocha, a drink that helps many people make it through the afternoon. Chocolate and coffee are also the basis for some of the most elegant desserts, such as chocolate-espresso cheese-cake and mousse.

CHOCOLATE AND CARAMEL

* * *

The union of these two mixtures, each of which combines the tastes of sweet and bitter in an unctuous substance, can bring tears to the eyes of chocolate lovers. Chocolate and caramel are the basis for a number of sublime chocolate pastries and desserts, and are mixed with pecans to make chocolate turtles, a cherished Midwestern candy.

CHOCOLATE AND MARSHMALLOW

* * *

The main ingredients for chocolate Easter eggs, rocky road candy, and its spin-off, rocky road ice cream.

1615:
ANNE OF AUSTRIA, DAUGHTER OF PHILIP III OF SPAIN, MARRIES LOUIS XIII AND BRINGS HIM SPANISH CHOCOLATE AS A GIFT. CHOCOLATE, WHICH HAD BEEN MONOPOLIZED BY SPAIN FOR ALMOST A CENTURY, SOON BECOMES THE RAGE OF THE FRENCH COURT.

CHOCOLATE AND SALT

* * *

Although this is not a twosome that immediately springs to mind, the combination of chocolate and salty food is dear to the heart of aficionados of chocolate covered pretzels, Reese's peanut butter cups, and peanut butter and chocolate fudge. A tiny pinch of salt is often added to chocolate desserts to heighten the sweetness and the taste of chocolate.

CHOCOLATE AND SPIRITS

* * *

Distilled spirits are one of the best companions for chocolate, both as flavorings for desserts and as fillings for chocolates and European candy bars. Rum, fruit brandies, and Cognac are some of the favorites. Chocolate should not be eaten with wine, as it will kill the taste of the wine; Armagnac, port, and Madeira, however, are strong enough to be served with a chocolate dessert.

CHOCOLATE AND VANILLA

* * *

It only seems right that the fruit of a tropical orchid should be the perfect partner for chocolate made from the beans of a tropical tree. Vanilla has been added to chocolate since both foods were first processed, and because it heightens the taste of chocolate and adds its own haunting perfume, it remains the favorite of all chocolate flavorings.

CHOCOLATE AND CHOCOLATE

* * *

To a true chocolate lover, chocolate mixed with chocolate is the best of all worlds, whether in the form of chocolate cookies or ice cream with chocolate chips, pastries that combine various chocolate fillings and toppings with chocolate génoise, or chocolate truffles with a coating of couverture.

1660:
THE PHYSICIAN TO QUEEN ANNE OF ENGLAND MIXES CHOCOLATE WITH MILK, A SECRET FORMULA THAT IS USED AS A RESTORATIVE. THE FRENCH PLANT COCOA TREES ON MARTINIQUE.

1690:
CHOCOLATE APPEARS IN GERMANY FOR THE FIRST TIME.

CHOCOLATE-CHERRY AMARETTI COOKIES

* * *

QUICK TO MAKE AND EASY TO STORE. FILL A TIN WITH THESE TANGY CHOCOLATE BITES, A THOUGHTFUL GIFT.

1 cup almond paste

1 egg white

4 teaspoons unsweetened cocoa powder

20 Italian dessert cherries in heavy syrup, drained and pitted

1/2 cup sliced almonds, coarsely chopped

Preheat oven to 350°F. Soften almond paste in mixing bowl with egg white. Add cocoa and mix well. Form balls the size of quarters by hand. Using your thumb, make an indent in each ball and stuff a cherry into it. Roll cookie in almonds. Place on baking sheet 2 inches apart and bake until almonds are lightly toasted, about 30 minutes. Makes about 20 cookies.

CHOCOLATE-PECAN PIE

* * *

THIS IS TRADITIONAL, SWEET, AND GOOEY.

4 eggs

1 cup dark corn syrup

1/3 cup sugar

2 ounces unsweetened chocolate, chopped

2 tablespoons unsalted butter

1/4 cup brewed coffee

1 1/2 cups whole pecan halves

One 9-inch deep-dish pie shell, unbaked

Preheat oven to 425°F. Mix eggs, corn syrup and sugar together. Do not overbeat. Melt chocolate and butter together. Add in coffee. Stir into egg mixture. Fold in pecans. Pour into unbaked pie shell.

Bake at 425°F for 10 minutes, then lower temperature to 375°F and bake for an additional 25 to 30 minutes until crust is golden and center is set. Makes one 9-inch pie.

No one has surpassed the Europeans for the elegance and sophistication of their chocolate desserts and candies. But the American love of chocolate has resulted in the creation of such homey and down-to-earth pleasures as brownies, banana splits, hot fudge sundaes, devil's food cake—named for its reddish brown color—and chocolate cream pie. It was American ingenuity in the person of Milton Hershey that made the chocolate bar a famous form of exchange and a symbol of affection around the world, not to mention Hershey's Kisses, Hershey's Syrup, and Hershey's Cocoa, all of which have made childhood sweeter for generations of Americans. In American hands, chocolate layer cake became not exquisite and refined, but a thing of ultimate and absolute chocolateness. And few desserts are more wonderful to the American palate than German chocolate cake, a tender, pale cocoa–colored cake topped with a mixture of shredded coconut, nuts, and sweetened condensed milk that is not German at all, but named after the German's Sweet Chocolate with which it is made.

1696:
THE MAYOR OF ZURICH VISITS BELGIUM AND BRINGS CHOCOLATE BACK TO SWITZERLAND.

Early 18th Century:
EMPEROR CHARLES VI OF AUSTRIA BRINGS CHOCOLATE TO VIENNA. BECAUSE IT IS NOT HIGHLY TAXED AS IN OTHER COUNTRIES, IT BECOMES POPULAR WITH THE COMMON PEOPLE AS WELL AS WITH THE COURT.

The cult of chocolate is manifested in widely scattered small temples devoted to the worship of this substance. Such temples can be found in large cities all over the world, but the most devoted cultists agree that the holiest of all of these is found in the city of Lyons in France, and its name is Bernachon. For only here is the ancient ritual of transformation reenacted in its entirety, beginning with the most basic element of the cult object, the small dried seeds of a tropical tree.

Unlike other temples, which create their cult objects from solid chocolate created at other holy sites, Bernachon garners the most precious of cocoa beans from countries near the great circle of the earth. The beans are heated by fire, at which point the chocolate incense rises and fills the sacred space of the temple. Then the beans are blended according to a secret alchemical formula and ground to a fine paste, and sugar, the black fruit of orchids, and a white waxy substance called cocoa butter are added. The mixture is again subjected to fire, after which it undergoes a secret three-day ceremony called the *conchage*, in which it is unceasingly rocked and caressed.

The substance is allowed to cool and harden before it is mixed with the incomparable butter and cream of France and shaped into symbolic forms. Finally, the objects are nestled in tiny cups, placed in precious containers of silver and gold marked with the name of Bernachon, and shipped by air to devotees in distant places, and the cult of chocolate is continued on the earth.

* * *

1765:
BAKER'S, THE FIRST FOOD COMPANY IN THE UNITED STATES AND THE FIRST TO MAKE CHOCOLATE
IN THE NEW WORLD, IS FOUNDED IN DORCHESTER, MASSACHUSETTS, BY DR. JAMES BAKER.

* * *

Here there is no nonfat cocoa, no skim milk, no *nourriture allegée* (light food) or *assiettes de régime* (diet plates), no small-minded concern with calories or mingy counting of fat grams. Surrounded by mirrors, marble, red carpeting, and gilded molding, in a very old tea salon built on the former site of the royal stables, the patrons of Angélina eat elaborately constructed pastries and sip hot chocolate as it was prepared in the carefree, sumptuous days of the Sun King: dense squares of rich bittersweet chocolate melted in hot whole milk, accompanied with bowls of ivory rosettes of whipped heavy cream. This is a place not of denial or restraint, but of indulgence and abandon, a place where butter and cream are honored for their ability to satisfy the body and the soul.

The patrons seated at the small round marble tables in this most Parisian place of faded Belle Époque elegance are a cross-section of a certain strata of the city: elegant elderly French people, beautifully dressed women of a certain age, the young *bon chic bon genre*, and tourists in the know. After they are served their pitcher of chocolate and bowl of cream, patrons pour their own chocolate into the white china cups decorated with the name of the shop. The hot chocolate, already so thick it leaves a dark path on the tongue of the pitcher, is then enriched by the addition of as many rosettes of whipped cream as one chooses to stir into the hot liquid. In a city famous for its temples of food and its elevation of chocolate to an art form, this is hot chocolate as it was taken in the morning by the pampered nobles and favorites of the royal court: luxurious, voluptuous, and guiltless.

* * *

1824:
JOHN CADBURY, AN ENGLISH QUAKER, BEGINS ROASTING AND GRINDING CHOCOLATE BEANS TO SELL IN HIS TEA AND COFFEE SHOP. MENIER OPENS THE FIRST CHOCOLATE FACTORY, NEAR PARIS.

1842:
CADBURY'S CHOCOLATE COMPANY IN ENGLAND CREATES THE FIRST CHOCOLATE BAR.

CHOCOLATE BUTTER COOKIES

* * *

BECAUSE WE STILL SAY "REMEMBER THOSE GREAT CHOCOLATE COOKIES GRANDMA USED TO MAKE."

2 ounces unsweetened chocolate, chopped

1 cup butter, softened to room temperature

1/2 cup powdered sugar

2 cups all-purpose flour

1/4 teaspoon salt

1/3 cup cornstarch

Melt chocolate in small heavy saucepan over low heat. Set aside to cool. Beat butter with sugar until mixture is light and fluffy. Beat in melted chocolate. In a separate bowl, sift together the flour, salt and cornstarch. Beat into butter mixture. Gather the dough into a ball. Divide in half and roll each into a log about 2 inches in diameter. Wrap in plastic and chill for at least 30 minutes.

Preheat oven to 325°F. Cut log into slices about 1/4 inch thick and place on an ungreased cookie sheet or on parchment. The tops of the cookies can be marked with the tines of a fork or baked plain. Bake for 15 minutes, or until set. Makes 4 dozen (cutting 1/4 inch thick from a 2-inch-thick log).

Chocolate is not only uniquely satisfying, but its availability allows for one of the greatest of all human pleasures, instant gratification. To a chocoholic, one of the primary indicators of an evolving world consciousness is the variety of forms of good chocolate available in his or her neighborhood.

A recent guidebook to fine chocolates provides an international list of chocolatiers, grading them with a system of stars, so that travelers can look up the best chocolates in any part of the United States and Europe. But you don't need to have access to Fauchon in Paris or La Maison du Chocolat in Paris or New York to buy good chocolate. As we approach the millennium, civilization in this country has advanced to such a degree that anyone can find chocolate almost anywhere and at any time. Twenty-four-hour drugstores have boxed candies and rows of candy bars, with new ones invented seemingly every month. Most big cities have their own local chocolate maker, as well as candy shops and department stores selling chocolates from a variety of chocolatiers, many of them from Europe. Every supermarket has not only candy and candy bars, but cocoa and chocolate for making your own treats at home, and fine European baking chocolate is now widely available in supermarkets and specialty foods stores. Restaurants, movie snack bars, mom-and-pop groceries, and gas stations sell chocolate—in fact, chocolate is impossible to avoid in our culture.

* * *

1852:
DOMINGO GHIRARDELLI, HAVING EARNED HIS CAPITAL SELLING GOODS TO MINERS IN THE CALIFORNIA GOLD RUSH, ENTERS THE CONFECTIONERY TRADE IN SAN FRANCISCO.

1857:
NEUHAUS, THE FIRST OF A LONG LINE OF BELGIAN CHOCOLATIERS, OPENS A SHOP IN BRUSSELS.

MEXICAN HOT CHOCOLATE

* * *

As unusual as it may seem, pepper and chocolate do work well together. This will truly warm you.

4 cups milk

2 ounces unsweetened chocolate, chopped

2 tablespoons sugar

1 teaspoon ground cinnamon

1/4 teaspoon black pepper, finely ground

Heat milk in medium-sized saucepan until hot. Add remaining ingredients and whisk until chocolate is melted and mixture is slightly foamy. Serve in warm cups. Serves 4.

MINT TEA WITH CHOCOLATE LEAVES

* * *

It's a good idea to serve these on a small chilled plate. You can drop them into your hot mint tea to melt, or eat them separately.

3 ounces semisweet chocolate, chopped

12 small camellia leaves (or other firm, waxy plant leaves)

4 cups steeped peppermint tea

To make chocolate leaves:
Melt chocolate. Using a small paintbrush, coat underside of leaves. Refrigerate leaves until ready to use. Gently peel leaf from chocolate and place chocolate on chilled plate. Serve with mint tea. Serves 4.

dark

IT SEEMS TO ME THAT OUR THREE BASIC NEEDS,

FOR FOOD AND SECURITY AND LOVE, ARE SO MIXED

AND MINGLED AND ENTWINED THAT WE CANNOT STRAIGHTLY

THINK OF ONE WITHOUT THE OTHERS.

SO IT HAPPENS THAT WHEN I WRITE OF HUNGER,

I AM REALLY WRITING ABOUT LOVE AND THE HUNGER FOR IT,

AND WARMTH AND THE LOVE OF IT AND

THE HUNGER FOR IT . . . AND THEN THE WARMTH AND

RICHNESS AND FINE REALITY OF HUNGER SATISFIED . . . AND

IT IS ALL ONE.

M. F. K. FISHER, FOREWORD TO *THE GASTRONOMICAL ME*

The list of things to which we can be addicted is a long one; it includes love, sex, drugs, alcohol, excitement, religion, worry, pain, and various kinds of food. Chocolate is one of the more benign addictions; as one writer has said, if you have to be addicted to something, it might as well be chocolate.

Like those other exotic dark foods, tea and coffee, chocolate was thought to have almost magical properties when it was introduced to Europe. At first it was suspect in some quarters because it was so unlike any other kind of food with which Europeans were familiar, but it soon became heralded as a restorative. The famous pairing of bread and chocolate was due partly to the belief that eating chocolate with bread made the chocolate more digestible, but also because it was thought that this combination equaled a fully nutritious meal.

1875:

A SWISS CHOCOLATE MAKER, DANIEL PETER, MIXES HENRI NESTLÉ'S CONDENSED MILK WITH CHOCOLATE, AND THE TWO MEN FOUND A COMPANY TO MANUFACTURE THE FIRST MILK CHOCOLATE.

HOT BUTTERED COGNAC WITH CHOCOLATE-DIPPED SPOONS

RELAXING AND DECADENT ON A COLD RAINY NIGHT, THIS WILL WARM YOU INSIDE AND OUT.

3 1/2 cups apple cider

6 whole cloves

1 tablespoon fresh lemon juice

1/2 cup Cognac

4 slices butter
   (about 1/4 inch thick)

3 ounces semisweet chocolate,
   chopped

Pour cider, cloves, and lemon juice into small saucepan. Bring to a boil. Pour into individual mugs, divide Cognac evenly among mugs, and top with a slice of butter. Serve with chocolate-dipped spoons for stirring.

To make spoons:
Melt chocolate in small bowl in a microwave oven (3 minutes on defrost). Dip 4 chilled spoons into melted chocolate about halfway up. Allow chocolate to cool before serving with Cognac. Slowly stir hot Cognac with a chocolate-coated spoon. Serves 4.

To the chocolate lover, happiness is a bar of French chocolate in the pantry. Sadly, this kind of happiness is as ephemeral as many others, for French chocolate tends to disappear rapidly from pantry shelves. That is why chocolate lovers think fondly of cocoa as their old reliable standby, the faithful companion they can count on when flashy European chocolate is not around. Unsweetened cocoa powder can be purchased as regular cocoa, low-fat cocoa, or Dutch cocoa, the latter prized by many bakers for its darker color and, some think, its more mellow flavor.

But for many of us, the dark-chocolate-brown rounded tin of Hershey's cocoa with its elongated silver lettering is a friend in time of need. Cocoa can be used to make lower-fat versions of many chocolate desserts, allowing the chocolate lover to indulge in the taste of chocolate without wallowing in guilt. (Most cocoas are from 10 to 24 percent fat, while reduced-fat cocoa has virtually no fat. Unsweetened chocolate, by contrast, can be as much as 56 percent fat.) A fine dusting of cocoa on a chocolate dessert and the rim of its plate creates instant elegance. At the other extreme, cocoa is the every-ready essential ingredient for the secret vice of many chocolate-lovers: homemade hot chocolate sauce eaten directly from the pan. Finally, of course, cocoa is the source for hot cocoa, that beloved late-night, early-morning, cold-winter-afternoon, cheer-you-up-on-a-grumpy-day, take-along-in-a-thermos-for-a-picnic-or-camping-trip, and cozy-the-children drink. Hot cocoa is the ultimate comfort beverage, a smooth, warm, perfumey elixir that will brighten any moment and gladden the heart of every chocolate lover.

* * *

1880:
RODOLPHE LINDT INVENTS THE MECHANICAL PROCESS KNOWN AS CONCHING, OR THE LONG KNEADING OF CHOCOLATE TO CREATE AN ESPECIALLY SMOOTH AND MELLOW SUBSTANCE.

The heartland of America excels in chocolate creations: brownies, devil's food cake, chocolate cupcakes, chocolate layer cake, chocolate cream pie, turtles, chocolate chip cookies, German chocolate cake, fudge, Bosco syrup, hot fudge sundaes. But only New York City claims the egg cream, a drink that epitomizes urban attitude by containing neither eggs nor cream, but instead chocolate syrup, milk, and soda water. Like New York, there's nothing else quite like it: It's surprising, fizzy, quirky, and unique.

* * *

Like mahogany, the best chocolate is a mixture of a deep wine-red undertone with a woody blackish brown. Now we give the name *chocolate* to creatures and foods whose peculiar red-brown color sets them apart from all others of their kind: chocolate Labrador retrievers, chocolate-point Siamese cats, chocolate bell peppers, chocolate cosmos flowers, and chocolate-colored tomatoes.

1894:
MILTON HERSHEY ADDS A LINE OF CHOCOLATE TO HIS CARAMEL MANU-
FACTURING BUSINESS. SOON HE INVENTS THE HERSHEY BAR BY EXPERI-
MENTING WITH MILK CHOCOLATE. HERSHEY'S COCOA APPEARS NEXT.

1896:
LEONARD HERSHFIELD
INVENTS THE TOOTSIE ROLL,
NAMED AFTER HIS DAUGHTER.

MOCHA RASPBERRIES

* * *

SERVE THREE OF THESE JEWELS WITH AN AFTER-DINNER COFFEE OR PORT.
THIS IS A SIMPLE DESSERT WITH NO EFFORT, JUST A LITTLE SWEETNESS.

12 chocolate-covered coffee beans

12 fresh raspberries

1/4 cup semisweet chocolate powder

Place a chocolate coffee bean in center of each raspberry. Roll raspberries lightly in chocolate powder. Serves 4.

CHOCOLATE - PISTACHIO BREAD

* * *

TRY THIS BREAD SLICED AND TOASTED WITH FRESH
FARMERS' CHEESE AND BUTTER PEAR. IT MAKES A WONDERFUL FRENCH TOAST
WITH A RASPBERRY SYRUP.

1/2 cup room temperature sweet butter

1 cup sugar

2 eggs

1 teaspoon vanilla extract

1 cup milk

2 cups all-purpose flour

1 1/2 teaspoons baking powder

1/2 teaspoon baking soda

1/2 teaspoon salt

1/3 cup unsweetened cocoa powder

1 cup pistachio nuts, chopped

Preheat oven to 350°F. Grease a 9-by-5-by-3-inch pan. Cream butter and sugar together until light and fluffy. Add eggs and vanilla, mixing well. Add milk. Sift the dry ingredients together. Add to the butter mixture, mixing well. Fold in pistachios. Pour mixture into the prepared pan. Bake for 1 hour and 15 minutes until top is lightly browned and wooded skewer comes out clean. Cool in pan for 10 minutes. Makes 1 loaf.

If desire has a taste, it must be the taste of chocolate: deep, fundamental, and intense. Those who love chocolate cannot explain their passion, anymore than we can explain why we are drawn to certain people, places, sounds, or scents that seem to awaken some old knowledge inside us, the kind of knowledge that is revealed to us in dreams. These strong affinities hint of lives already lived in some other time and place, and who can say beyond all doubt that chocolate lovers were not once warriors in the Mayan rain forests, or nobles in the Spanish court?

Chocolate, like any form of passion, seduces us by its uniqueness. When we long for chocolate, no other taste will do. Its singular flavor, its silken texture like that of human skin, its sensuous melting in response to human body temperature combine to promise us that, in a world where we so often don't get what we want, chocolate will be a faithful lover.

* * *

Some Valentine's gifts, like gold or diamonds, are meant to symbolize the enduring quality of love; others, like flowers or candy, signify the almost unbearable sweetness of temporality. Like love, chocolate is a thing of paradoxes: exotic but elemental, forbidden but familiar, dangerous but comforting, dark but warm, bitter and sweet at the same time. What could be a more perfect token for any romance than a red heart-shaped box of chocolates—the color of passion and the shape of the source of deep emotion—each cunningly shaped and carefully presented in its own pleated chocolate-colored paper cup or tissue-thin gold or silver foil wrapper: so many sweet moments, waiting to be consumed.

* * *

1897:
BROWNIES ARE FIRST MENTIONED IN PRINT, LISTED FOR
SALE IN THE SEARS, ROEBUCK AND CO. CATALOGUE. CADBURY BEGINS TO
MANUFACTURE MILK CHOCOLATE IN COMPETITION WITH THE SWISS.

1899:
JEAN TOBLER, A SWISS, BEGINS
MANUFACTURING CHOCOLATE.

Chocolate is valued not only for its taste and shining surface and its crisp yet yielding texture, but for its ability to be used in an almost infinite number of ways. It has an affinity with an amazing range of sweet, sour, bitter, and salty foods, and can be used in both sweet and savory dishes. Its texture can be altered with the addition of cream, butter, eggs, and other ingredients; it can be used to coat almost anything; it is used to flavor baked goods, as a filling, and as icing.

Best of all, to pastry chefs and confectioners, chocolate is a protean substance that can be shaped into almost any form that the imagination can create: Eiffel towers, Easter bunnies, Santas, letters of the alphabet, sea urchins—the list is endless. Chocolate owes its mutability to its cocoa-butter content, for cocoa butter melts at 92°F, or just below body temperature; thus chocolate can be tempered, molded, and dipped to any fanciful design or configuration, then remain intact until eaten. Because women have a slightly slower metabolism and thus a lower body temperature than do men, women are preferred as the makers of hand-dipped chocolates, those artful objects of desire that melt in our mouth.

About 1900:
A MACHINE CALLED THE ENROBER IS INVENTED TO REPLACE THE TASK OF HAND-DIPPING CHOCOLATE.

1903:
MILTON HERSHEY BUYS THE LAND FOR THE FUTURE FACTORY AND TOWN OF HERSHEY, PENNSYLVANIA. THE HERSHEY BAR SOON BECOMES WORLD FAMOUS.

CHOCOLATE-ZINFANDEL SAUCE

* * *

THIS WARM AND SAVORY SAUCE IS WONDERFUL WITH ROASTED OR GRILLED MEATS. SERVE WITH LAMB, PORK, OR GRILLED CHICKEN.

3 whole cloves

6 black peppercorns

One 2-inch stick cinnamon

1 teaspoon cumin seed

1/2 teaspoon cardamom

2 cups zinfandel wine

2 tablespoons packed brown sugar

1 cup dried pitted sour cherries

1 ounce unsweetened chocolate, chopped

4 tablespoons butter

1/2 cup good-quality beef stock

Toast the cloves, peppercorns, cinnamon, cumin seed, and cardamom in a heavy saucepan, stirring about 3 minutes until all are hot and aroma released. Add the zinfandel and brown sugar, and simmer until reduced by half, about 20 minutes. When zinfandel is reduced, remove saucepan from heat and add cherries. Let soak while you prepare the rest of the ingredients.

In a small saucepan, melt the chocolate and butter. Whisk the beef stock into the chocolate and heat. Add the spiced zinfandel and keep warm until served. Makes enough sauce for 4 servings.

Cocoa trees love warmth and moisture, thus they will grow only in a band within ten to twenty degrees of the equator. Within this band are a number of varieties of cocoa trees, each bred for a different microclimate. Cocoa trees love sunlight, but it must be filtered, so they grow beneath the canopy of large trees such as banana and papaya; on cocoa plantations these trees are referred to as "cocoa mothers."

Nothing about a cocoa tree gives the slightest indication that it is the source of chocolate. The short trees with their large tropical leaves have some rather otherworldly traits: The tiny star-shaped white flowers bud and bloom directly from the trunk and sometimes the largest branches of the tree, because the large pods they develop into are too heavy to be borne by most of the branches. The trees flower and fruit simultaneously and continuously, and each foot-long pod protrudes randomly from the trunk. Ridged and blunt-ended, the pods are beautifully colored in the whole range of the tropical palette, depending on ripeness and variety: chartreuse, mango, papaya, pale aubergine, banana, deep magenta, orange, green-golden, and clear bright red. Inside them is a sweet white edible pulp and, enmeshed in a white spongy substance at the core, the rounded white, pale purple, or deep purple seeds.

Right after being picked, the pods are held for several days to allow the seeds, or beans, to ferment; then they are removed from the pods and spread out in the sun to dry. Finally, the beans are put into sacks and sent to chocolate manufacturers around the world to be blended with other varieties of beans and to begin the long, exacting process of being transformed into fine chocolate.

* * *

1907:
HERSHEY'S KISSES ARE
ADDED TO THE COMPANY'S
LINE OF CHOCOLATES.

1908:
TOBLERONE IS INVENTED BY THEODOR TOBLER
AS A COMBINATION OF CHOCOLATE AND TORRONE,
IN THE TRIANGULAR SHAPE OF ALPINE PEAKS.

CHOCOLATE SOUFFLÉ

* * *

A SOUFFLÉ IS ALWAYS AN IMPRESSIVE ENDING TO A MEAL.
THIS IS A CHOCOLATE CLASSIC.

1 tablespoon melted butter

4 ounces bittersweet chocolate

1/2 cup heavy cream

2 teaspoons extrafine ground coffee beans or good-quality coffee crystals

3 eggs, separated

2 tablespoons brandy

1/2 teaspoon vanilla extract

3 tablespoons extrafine sugar

Confectioners' sugar

Preheat the oven to 425°F and place the rack in the lower third of the oven, providing enough room for the soufflé to rise. Brush the soufflé dish with the melted butter and set aside. Coarsely chop the chocolate with a chefs' knife and then process finely in a food processor. In a medium saucepan, combine the chocolate and cream, stirring until melted and smooth, about 5 minutes. Add the coffee beans or coffee crystals. Remove from the heat.

Add the egg yolks, one at a time, whisking constantly until combined with the chocolate. Simmer about 4 minutes. Remove from the heat and whisk in the brandy and vanilla.

At this point you can refrigerate the mixture for up to 4 hours, tightly covered. Reheat just until hot to the touch, stirring till smooth.

Beat the egg whites until stiff. Continue beating while adding the extrafine sugar. The mixture should become glossy in about 30 seconds. Fold a small amount of the egg whites into the chocolate until it is a thin consistency and then fold in the rest of the whites, taking care not to overwork the batter. Gently fill the prepared soufflé dish and bake until puffed, about 15 to 20 minutes. Sprinkle decoratively with confectioners' sugar, using a cut template or a sieve or shaker. Serve immediately. Serves 2 to 4.

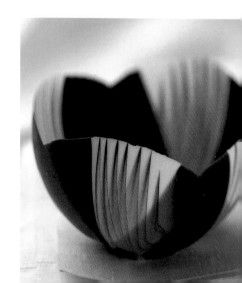

bittersweet

IF CHOCOLATE

BLACK SHINING

GLAZED THIN, CRACKED LIKE A FROST

ICE SHEET

THE SQUARE PAN COOLS, THE KNIFE GRATES

INTO SUGAR CRYSTALLIZED, INTO WARM

DAMP PARTICLES, BLACK DEEP

SEPARATE, THE NUTS ARE SOLID

AND THE MIDDLE IS ALMOST LIQUID

BLACKER. BALL

A CRUMB ON YOUR FINGER.

SALTY CHOCOLATE IS SWEETER,

AND THE MIXING SPOON IS ROUGH

TO LICK, SALTY.

GROUND COFFEE,

BITTER, FULL BROWN-BLACK

IN THE THROAT, AND

CHOCOLATE FLOATS LOW IN THE KITCHEN.

*

"IF CHOCOLATE," SUSAN HERRON SIBBET, FROM *BURNT TOAST AND OTHER RECIPES*

Today, coffee, cola, tea, sugar, and tobacco are found all over the world. The cooking of Europe and the Americas are unthinkable without the native foods that those continents have adopted from one another, and African and Asian foods are an important part of North American cooking. Now, even in Asia, a homesick American can find a chocolate bar to give comfort in a foreign land.

* * *

The Greek gods feasted on ambrosia, a mysterious food unknown to mortal beings. But in the New World, the food of the gods grew in the knotted greenness of the rain forest, hidden inside an oblong, golden-green pulpy fruit that emerged from the trunk of a certain short tree. Although the gods of Mount Olympus were petty and often cruel, the Amerindian gods far surpassed them in their cruelty, for they demanded continual offerings of human, rather than animal, blood. As if in exchange, they shared all their bounty with the human world. Quetzalcoatl himself, the god of the forest, gave mortals the cocoa tree, which was so highly valued by them that its seeds were used as coins.

1911:
MILTON HERSHEY INVENTS A CHOCOLATE BAR MADE WITH
HYDROGENATED VEGETABLE OIL IN PLACE OF COCOA BUTTER
TO PREVENT ITS MELTING IN WARM CLIMATES.

1914:
HERSHEY BARS ARE INCLUDED
IN THE RATIONS OF AMERICAN
SOLDIERS IN WORLD WAR I.

WHITE CHOCOLATE AND LIME TART

* * *

THIS IS SURPRISINGLY LIGHT AND BEAUTIFUL, WITH CHOCOLATE SHAVINGS AND LIME ZEST SPRINKLED OVER TOP—TRULY SWEET AND TART TOGETHER.

Graham Cracker Crust:

6 tablespoons melted butter, plus 1 tablespoon softened to coat pan

8 ounces graham crackers

1/4 cup sugar

4 ounces bittersweet chocolate, melted

Filling:

3/4 cup heavy cream

1/2 cup milk

12 ounces white chocolate, chopped, plus shavings for garnish

Grated zest of 2 limes, julienned zest of 1

Juice from 3 limes

Bittersweet chocolate shavings for garnish

To make crust:

Preheat oven to 350°F. Coat a 10-inch tart pan with the softened butter. Process the crackers and sugar in food processor to a fine texture. Add the melted butter and process to combine. Press crumb mixture evenly in bottom and up sides of pan. Bake about 7 minutes, or until golden brown.

Pour melted chocolate into the crust, and using a rubber spatula, spread to cover the bottom and sides of the crust evenly. Let cool to harden the chocolate before filling.

To make filling:

Heat cream and milk to just below simmering. Add chocolate and grated lime zest. Stir until all chocolate is melted and add lime juice. Set aside to cool. Pour and level into a prepared, chocolate-lined crust. Refrigerate until firm. Garnish with julienned zest and both white and dark chocolate shavings. Serves 8.

WARM CHOCOLATE RISOTTO

* * *

THIS IS BEST EATEN WARM FROM A BOWL. CHOCOLATE COMFORT FOOD.

1 cup arborio rice

2 cups water

4 cups half-and-half, heated

6 ounces bittersweet chocolate, chopped

1 tablespoon vanilla extract

2 tablespoons sugar

Combine rice and water in a large saucepan and bring to a boil. Reduce heat and stir frequently until almost all the liquid has been absorbed.

Gradually add 1/2 cup of half-and-half and stir frequently until half-and-half is almost all absorbed. Repeat with the remaining half-and-half, 1/2 cup at a time. At the last 1/2 cup addition add the chocolate, vanilla, and the sugar, stirring constantly until most of the half-and-half has been absorbed and the rice is tender. Serves 4 to 6.

Chocolate used alone, as a coating or lining, or as a material for decorations, needs to be handled with special care. Melted chocolate will lose flavor and texture if its temperature exceeds 120°F, and it may not set properly if the temperature of the room exceeds 74°F. Ideally, the room temperature should be between 65° and 70°F, and the air should be neither drafty nor humid. All water, including steam, must be kept away from melted chocolate to prevent it from suddenly stiffening to a hard mass, an action known as "seizing." Tempering chocolate prevents bloom, the white powderlike coating caused by excessive heat or humidity; it also creates chocolate that is more malleable and has a brighter shine, a fuller flavor, and a sharp "snap" when the chocolate is bitten.

The best chocolate for coating is couverture, which has a higher percentage of cocoa butter than regular chocolate, allowing it to be more easily molded and to be poured into an especially thin layer for coating. The process of tempering consists of raising the temperature of chocolate in order to break down the structure of the cocoa butter crystals, then cooling it to re-create that structure. When the chocolate sets, the crystals join in perfect chains, creating a shiny, clean-breaking coating.

To temper chocolate, melt it in a double boiler over not-quite-simmering water (about 120°F). Don't let the bottom of the chocolate container touch the water as the chocolate melts, and stir the chocolate occasionally until it has melted and reached a temperature of 100°F. Remove the chocolate from heat and let it cool to within one or two degrees of 90°F, or until a tiny bit dabbed on your upper lip feels cool. Chocolate can be cooled by simply letting it sit, by pouring it out on a marble slab or metal pan, by adding solid chocolate to the melted chocolate and stirring it until melted, or by stirring it to lower the temperature.

1920:

FANNY FARMER CHOCOLATE SHOPS, NAMED IN HONOR OF COOKBOOK AUTHOR FANNIE FARMER, ARE FOUNDED. THE WHITMAN COMPANY INTRODUCES THE WHITMAN SAMPLER, COMPLETE WITH A CHART SHOWING EACH KIND OF CANDY IN THE BOX, AND MARKETS IT IN DRUGSTORES.

To maintain the chocolate at the proper temperature, place the bowl over tepid water or on a heating pad set on low. If the chocolate inadvertently becomes too cool, it can be rewarmed to 90°F, but if the temperature goes over 90°F, the chocolate will lose its temper and must be cooled again to 90°F.

* * *

Melting chocolate is a delicate affair, as it can be ruined by being over-heated or by allowing water to touch it. When a recipe calls for chocolate to be melted, first chop the chocolate into small pieces with a French chef's knife. If you have a heat deflector, melt the chocolate in a heavy pan set on the deflector over low heat. Otherwise, use a double boiler over not-quite-simmering water. If you don't have a double boiler, use a ceramic or stainless steel bowl set over a pan of not-quite-simmering water; take care that the bottom of the bowl does not touch the water. Dark chocolate should be stirred occasionally as it melts, while milk chocolate should be stirred very frequently. White chocolate, which is high in milk solids, must be stirred constantly while melting.

If the recipe calls for chocolate to be melted with butter or a liquid such as cream, simply warm the mixture over low heat, stirring it until the chocolate is melted. Or, if you like, you may melt the butter or heat the liquid first, then add the chocolate and stir to melt.

* * *

1921: PETER PAUL HALIJIAN INVENTS THE MOUNDS BAR, AND OTTO SCHNERING INVENTS THE BABY RUTH, NAMED AFTER PRESIDENT GROVER CLEVELAND'S DAUGHTER.

1923: H. B. REESE, A FORMER EMPLOYEE OF HERSHEY'S, BEGINS MAKING REESE'S PEANUT BUTTER CUPS.

CHOCOLATE - PUMPKIN PIE

* * *

THIS PIE WILL BE ONE OF THE REASONS YOU LOOK FORWARD TO FALL.

Pie filling:

2 ounces semisweet chocolate, grated

2 cups pumpkin purée

3 eggs, lightly beaten

1/2 cup heavy cream

1/2 cup packed brown sugar

1/2 teaspoon ground cinnamon

1/2 teaspoon ground ginger

1/2 teaspoon ground nutmeg

One 8-inch pie shell

For garnish:

1 cup toasted pumpkin seeds

Cinnamon-dusted whipped cream

Preheat oven to 375°F. Set aside half of the grated chocolate. Combine remaining ingredients for pie filling and stir until well blended. Pour into unbaked pie shell. Sprinkle remainder of grated chocolate evenly over pie filling. Bake for 50 to 55 minutes, or until pie filling is set and crust is golden brown. Sprinkle with toasted pumpkin seeds and allow pie to cool before serving with whipped cream and cinnamon. Makes one 8-inch pie. (This recipe can be divided into individual 4-inch tart pans to serve 6.)

CHOCOLATE AND LEMON ANGEL FOOD CAKE

THIS CAKE, WITH ITS FLECKS OF LEMON AND CHOCOLATE, IS LIGHT, SOFT, AND LOW IN FAT.

1 1/4 cups sugar

1 cup cake flour

1/2 teaspoon salt

12 egg whites at room
   temperature

1 teaspoon cream of tartar

1 teaspoon vanilla extract

4 ounces bittersweet chocolate,
   grated

1/3 cup grated lemon zest
   (about 7 lemons)

Preheat oven to 350°F. Sift 1/4 cup of the sugar and the flour and salt 3 times. Beat egg whites until foamy. Sprinkle cream of tartar over top, then beat until soft peaks form. Beat in the vanilla. Beat in the remaining sugar, 1 tablespoon at a time. Egg whites should look stiff and glossy. Mix chocolate and lemon zest into flour mixture. Fold the flour mixture into the egg whites. Pour into an ungreased 10-inch tube pan. Bake for 50 minutes, or until cake springs back when touched. Serves 6 to 8.

What makes the best chocolate? As with any food, the best ingredients are the first step. Most fine chocolate is made from a blend of different kinds of cacao beans; the specific blend varies according to the taste of the chocolatier. By far the most common type of cacao bean is forastero (meaning "foreign"); although it is disease-resistant and high-yielding, it has a poor flavor and makes chocolate with a rubbery texture. The rarest beans have the finest flavor; they are criollo (meaning "native") beans from Central America. Another kind of cacao, not quite as scarce as criollo, is trinitario, a hybrid of forastero and criollo developed on the island of Trinidad. Ecuador produces the best forastero beans, while most of the best criollo beans are cultivated in the Caribbean region, especially in Venezuela, which is attempting to increase its production of such fine varieties as Rio Caribe, Chuao, and Carenero. Central American and Caribbean beans are prized for their perfumes, variously described as resembling those of white flowers, dried fruit, caramel, and hazelnuts or almonds.

The beans are fermented and dried where they are grown, then are sent on to the manufacturer for roasting and grinding into a paste called chocolate or cocoa liquor, or cocoa mass. Extra cocoa butter, sugar, vanilla, and sometimes a very small amount of lecithin are now added to the chocolate liquor, and the mixture is conched, or mixed, continually to create a smooth texture and fine flavor. Aside from the quality and blend of the beans, and the care taken in fermenting and roasting, the most important factor in the creation of fine chocolate is the length of time it is conched. Times range from less than a day for cheap chocolate, to three to five days for the most silken chocolate.

1930:
FRANKLIN MARS INVENTS
THE SNICKERS BAR.

1939:
NESTLÉ INTRODUCES SEMISWEET
CHOCOLATE MORSELS.

1940s:
GI CHOCOLATE BECOMES A
MEDIUM OF EXCHANGE
IN WORLD WAR II EUROPE.

Unlike the best chocolate, inferior chocolate has a higher proportion of sugar to chocolate liquor, uses only forestero beans, replaces pure vanilla extract with artificial vanilla, or vanillin, and sometimes replaces much of the cocoa butter with hydrogenated vegetable oil. The cocoa content of chocolate is the primary indication of its quality; the finest chocolate contains 60 to 70 percent cocoa, and will list the content on the label.

Although fine chocolate is made in the United States, Germany, Italy, and Switzerland, and each of these countries has made important, and sometimes crucial, contributions to the development of chocolate, what is arguably the best chocolate comes from France. The best chocolates are also the freshest; ideally they should be eaten within one week of the time they are made. The most elegant chocolates are dipped (by hand or by machine), not molded, which yields the thinnest and most delicate of coatings. The quality of the interior is almost as important as the exterior; the best ones have the finest and lightest of fillings. Many chocolatiers continue to make traditional fillings such as vanilla- or liqueur-flavored ganache or praline, while others specialize in unusual flavors such as green tea, bergamot, and black currant.

In all of these things the French excel, as well as in the skill of creating cunning and exquisite shapes of chocolates, which are also beautifully packaged. Some names from this stellar rank of chocolatiers are Bernachon (Lyons), unique in making their own chocolate from scratch; Michel Chaudun (Paris and Tokyo); Debauve & Gallais, the oldest *chocolaterie* in Paris; Fauchon (Paris); Jean-Paul Hévin (Paris); and La Maison du Chocolat (Paris and New York).

1940:
THE MARS COMPANY INVENTS M&M'S FOR SOLDIERS GOING TO WORLD WAR II.

1947:
HALIJIAN INVENTS THE ALMOND JOY.

Post World War II:
GODIVA CHOCOLATES BEGIN TO BE MANUFACTURED IN BRUSSELS.

When chocolate is melted, or cocoa is dissolved into a paste, then mixed with eggs, flour, sugar, and some kind of liquid, a series of pleasures are set in motion. The first is the smooth viscous mixture that is high on any true chocolate lover's list: chocolate batter. However much we may love the taste of batter coating the spoon and the bowl, though, this cool raw material of chocolate cookies, cupcakes, and cakes is only the promise of more pleasures to come. Halfway through the baking process, the heavy fragrance of baking chocolate begins to emanate from the oven and fill the kitchen and the house, the scent so intense it seems that we can almost see it. At last, warm, dense, and yielding, cooling on a wire rack and waiting to be eaten, is the prize itself: dark, honeycombed, tender-crumbed, and risen.

1957:
A DALLAS NEWSPAPER PUBLISHES A RECIPE FOR
GERMAN CHOCOLATE CAKE MADE WITH GERMAN'S SWEET CHOCOLATE,
NAMED FOR ENGLISHMAN SAM GERMAN.

1995:
HÄAGEN-DAZS INTRODUCES NONFAT
CHOCOLATE SORBET.

CHOCOLATE GRANITA

* * *

THIS IS THE "GROWN-UP" VERSION OF FUDGCICLES AND FROZEN ORANGES,
ALL IN AN EASY, ENVIRONMENTALLY FRIENDLY SERVING DISH.

3 oranges

3 cups water

1 cup sugar

1 cup half-and-half

**1/4 cup unsweetened cocoa
powder**

**3 tablespoons Grand Marnier,
plus some to garnish serving**

Hollow out orange halves and chop fruit for garnish. Wrap the orange halves in plastic wrap and set in the freezer. Combine water, sugar, and half-and-half in a saucepan over medium heat. Stir until mixture is about to boil and all the sugar dissolved. Sift cocoa into a separate bowl. Add the 3 tablespoons Grand Marnier and stir in 1/3 cup of heated liquid mixture. Add to saucepan and mix well. Cool to room temperature. Pour into a shallow pan (such as an 8-inch cake pan) and set in freezer until frozen, at least 4 hours. Set in refrigerator 30 minutes to soften. Scoop granita into frozen orange halves. Garnish with orange chunks and a splash of Grand Marnier. Makes 1 quart, or 6 servings.

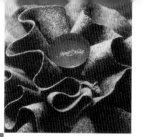

glossary

BALLOTIN

*

The French word for an elegant box filled with chocolates.

BITTERSWEET CHOCOLATE

*

Chocolate liquor to which sugar, cocoa butter, lecithin, and usually vanilla has been added. It has less sugar and usually more chocolate liquor than semisweet chocolate, but is interchangeable with it in cooking. European chocolate is generally bittersweet chocolate, while American chocolate is semisweet.

BLOOM

*

There are two causes for bloom, the white, powderlike blotches that sometimes appear on chocolate. Sugar bloom is caused by excessive humidity; when the moisture on the chocolate evaporates, the sugar can leach out of the chocolate and form crystals on the surface. Excessive heat causes fat bloom, which occurs when cocoa butter crystals melt and then re-form on the surface of the chocolate. Bloom affects the appearance but not the taste of chocolate.

BONBON

*

Literally "good good," because one good is not enough to describe it: a dipped or molded chocolate with a fondant filling that may include nuts or fruit.

CACAO

*

The Spanish word for cocoa; it is used interchangably with cocoa to refer to both the trees and the beans.

CHOCOLATE LIQUOR

*

Also called cocoa liquor, this is a paste created by crushing cocoa nibs. Baking, or bitter chocolate, is pure chocolate liquor.

CLUB DES CROQUERS DE CHOCOLAT

*

Literally, "the munchers-of-chocolate club," a French society of chocolate lovers.

COCOA CONTENT

*

The percentage of the net weight of chocolate or cocoa liquor (the American term) or cocoa solids (the European term) in chocolate. The cocoa content of the best chocolate is between 60 and 70 percent.

COCOA DANCE

*

The shuffling movement of Trinidadian women walking over cocoa beans to turn them so they will dry evenly.

COCOA MOTHERS

*

Tall trees, such as plantain and banana, planted to shield the shorter cocoa trees from direct sun.

COCOA NIBS

*

Skinned or shucked cocoa beans. They are 53 percent cocoa butter and 47 percent dry matter, or cocoa mass.

COCOA POWDER

*

Chocolate liquor that has had almost all the cocoa butter pressed out of it, yielding a cake that is then ground into cocoa. Most cocoas have at least 22 percent cocoa butter, but lower-fat cocoa is now available in some specialty foods and natural foods stores.

COCOA WALKS

*

Orchards of cocoa trees.

COMPOUND COATING

*

A combination of low-fat cocoa powder, sugar, and hydrogenated vegetable fat, used to coat chocolates.

CONCHING

*

The process of mechanically kneading and mixing chocolate to create a smooth texture and better flavor (the aeration of the chocolate lessens bitterness and increases aroma). Named after *concha*, or "shell," in Spanish; chocolate was originally kneaded and mixed by hand in shell-shaped troughs. The process is called *conchage* in French.

CONFECTIONERY COATINGS

*

Summer coating and compound coating, which are used in place of the more expensive couverture.

COUVERTURE

*

Chocolate with extra cocoa butter (usually at least 32 percent cocoa butter, and often more) added in order to make shiny, flavorful, and thin coatings for candies, cakes, and so on. Couverture is usually available only through bakers' supply houses or by mail order. It is sometimes called coating chocolate, but should not be confused with compound coating, an inferior product that does not contain chocolate liquor. Couverture chocolate needs to be handled with special care; see page 72.

CRU

*

Literally, "growth," referring to beans from a particular plantation.

CUVÉE

*

A blend of cocoa beans.

DUTCH COCOA

*

Cocoa that has been processed with alkali, a soluble salt, to raise the pH level of the cocoa beans. Because the natural acidity of the beans is neutralized by this process, Dutch cocoa is slightly milder in taste and deeper in color than regular cocoa. It is so named because the process was invented by a Dutchman. Devil's food cake owes its dark reddish brown color to the same chemical interaction, caused by the addition of baking soda, also an alkali, to the batter.

ENROBING

*

To coat a chocolate filling by dipping it or pouring chocolate over it, either mechanically or by hand.

GANACHE

*

A mixture of chocolate and heavy cream or crème fraîche. One of the basic chocolatier mixtures, ganache is used to fill and coat pastries and chocolates; it is the filling for chocolate truffles.

MILK CHOCOLATE

*

A combination of dry milk solids, sugar, cocoa butter, lecithin, and flavorings.

MOLINILLO

*

"Little mill," the ridged wooden stick that is spun in Mexican hot chocolate to beat it to a froth.

PALET D'OR

*

"Disk of gold," a French chocolate that consists of a thin one-inch-diameter disk of dark chocolate filled with ganache and topped with flecks of edible gold foil.

PRALINE

*

A basic filling for chocolates, praline (*praliné* in French) is made by roasting almonds or hazelnuts, then pouring caramel over the nuts. After the mixture hardens, it is crushed to a smooth paste.

SEIZING

*

The sudden stiffening of melted chocolate into an unworkable mass, caused by the introduction of water. If this happens when you are melting chocolate, add a few drops of vegetable oil to the chocolate, which will allow it to relax enough that other ingredients can be mixed in.

SEMISWEET CHOCOLATE

*

Similar to bittersweet chocolate, except that it has more sugar and usually less chocolate liquor. See Bittersweet Chocolate.

SUMMER COATING

*

A combination of dry milk solids, sugar, and hydrogenated vegetable oil, this material is used to coat chocolate when the room temperature exceeds 74°F, as it melts at a higher temperature than couverture chocolate or white chocolate. Summer coating is sometimes tinted in pastel colors and is often confused with white chocolate.

SWEET CHOCOLATE

*

This chocolate has more sugar and less chocolate liquor than semisweet chocolate.

TEMPERING

*

Melting and cooling chocolate to certain temperatures to create a shiny, flavorful, and thin coating for pastries and chocolates. For more on tempering, see page 72.

TRUFFLES

*

Misshapen chocolates made by hand of ganache and coated with cocoa powder to look like real truffles. Professional chocolate truffles are coated with couverture and so do not have to be refrigerated like homemade ones, but they should be refrigerated to keep them fresh if they are not eaten immediately. The larger, molded American version of truffles are shaped like haystacks.

UNSWEETENED CHOCOLATE

*

Pure chocolate liquor, also known as bitter chocolate or baking chocolate.

WHITE CHOCOLATE

*

Cocoa butter mixed with dry milk, sugar, and vanilla or vanillin.

XOCOLATL

*

"Bitter water," the Aztec word for drinking chocolate.

RECIPE LIST: